HOLD THAT THOUGHT

a book of inspiration, miracles and
empowerment

MARK BAJERSKI

INTRODUCTION

"My heart has been longing for the day when I will conquer my mountain. Today is that day and I have finally found what I was searching for." – Mark Bajerski

After I wrote my book, 'Diary of an Accidental Psychic', I was overwhelmed by the reaction of readers thanking me for sharing the divine experiences of many people who have come to me for healing. The true accounts about the magical healing power of synchronicity and the many divine interventions that occurred in the lives of people from all walks of life, brought much hope and a greater understanding of how Spirit, the Universe, is constantly giving us messages and signs to help us on our journey.

We are all deserving of love, peace and happiness and the place most essential to finding all the happiness intended for us is – within.

In this, my first pocket book of miracles and empowerment, I have brought together a collection of powerful messages from Spirit, which is intended, for each and every one of us.

On reflection of each message, I discover my light, my way and inner voice. In these moments of stilling my mind and opening my heart to these words, I find my strength, my purpose and my determination to keep climbing my mountain. I find focus to do what is intended for me and learn to let go of issues that only we allow to burden our lives.

My prayer is that you will also feel the power of these words from Spirit; that they will heal your world, remind you of all the strength you hold within and of the beauty that you bring to this world. How essential you are to the Universe.

My hope is that you will shine your light even brighter through these pages of light and love, to feel, to heal and to digest each empowering thought that takes you to new paths and greater adventures with each giant leap of faith.

My pure intention is that this pocket book of thoughts can be used in a wonderful and inspirational way. Perhaps each day you might like to choose a way to ask Spirit to show you your message on one (or more) of the pages. Close your eyes and open the book at a page that tells you to stop, look for the first number you see on your daily travels and open the book on this page - find a way that is magical to you and, through these practices, you are already finding your deeper connection to Spirit.

Most of all, feel the love intended for you in each message and live your life with the deepest sense of love and gratitude.

"Everything is as it should be. Where you are, is exactly where you are meant to be."
– Mark Bajerski

TEARS – by Arlene C

Dedicated to Mark Bajerski, my friend and healer of hearts.

I am joyful now.
Ever since that day you held my hand in
yours
And whispered in my ear,
"Allow your tears to fall without a care for
them.
Know that they flow from the heart.
The very origin of your being – the es-
sence of you.
Tears that are your own.
Your pain, joy, celebration, sorrows.
It is all of life like a river flowing through
you.
Each drop, releasing that part of your
beautiful story."

I am joyful now.
Knowing that my tears are as much a part
of me as I am of them.
Symbolising my deepest connection to
the Universe.
To life, to death and to all moments
in-between.
My heart, the source from which my
story flows;
I understand why my tears must always be
allowed to flow.
In each drop I show the world how much
I care, I love, I feel.
And I heal.
And I am joyful now.

Love, strength, self worth, inner peace, inner beauty, inner trust …
If you could hold on to these words that fill your heart with happiness, would you? And the vision to always see your inner gifts; if you could, would you hold on to that vision?
Then here - take my mirror and see everything that lies within you.

When you understand that you are not here to sacrifice your life for others, you begin to feel inner strength.
When you understand that this is your life, then you will receive an inner strength.
When you stop living other people's lives', you become free to live your own!
It's your life ... begin today!

Sometimes what we preach most is what we need most.

Spirit flows through our hearts and if we just stop and listen to our own voice, sometimes, just sometimes we may hear our own lessons.

The way to happiness begins within.
Remember who you are; remember all the amazing things you have done for your friends, family and loved ones, from when you were young up until to today.
Once you tune into this amazing energy you will recognise who you are and how amazing you truly are.

Trust is the key to opening doors you can't yet see!

Step out of the door today - it does not matter which way you go, left or right, the light shines bright either way.
See life like this each day and you will never again suffer from indecision.

The most beautiful colour of blue is all around you. This is your day to fly free, to step out of your door and fly.

Feel the freedom you dream about, waking each day in control of your destiny, never to be imprisoned or tied up.

Today be like a bird in the sky and do not allow time to control your beautiful life.

This is your moment to master time. Do not allow the feelings of impatience to take over your beautiful life ever again.

We all have gifts and talents that have a purpose in helping others. Many people are working for the higher good of mankind. Even in the darkest places of the world, if we hold a divine message that will help others gain or reawaken their faith, Spirit will find a way for that message to be heard.

The secret to walking a path of happiness is to surround yourself with beautiful people who love you and who you can love back with no judgment over one another.

If you get angry with me and I get angry with you, how can we make the anger stop?

It takes a stronger, more loving person to break this pattern.

It takes a caring and understanding person free from pride or ego to let go.

Never be the weaker one, for this will only keep you trapped in anger and pain.

Everything you need is right where you are standing.

It's never too late to say "Sorry".
To look at yourself and recognise your actions is indeed a great thing; a lesson which we all need to conquer.
Learn to apologise, not only to others but also to yourself.
We all make mistakes.

When we have darkness within, we can become addicted to many things.
When we have light within, there is no need for any addiction.
Darkness cannot stay where light shines.

There are times when we feel our family is judging us on many levels. Take heart and know that they are not being judgmental, nor are they being opinionated or controlling.

At times our loved ones are limited by their own understanding of how they feel your life should be.

This doesn't mean they don't love you - they love you the only way they know how.

Do not live to other people's limits. Be the higher energy and let go of any negative emotions and instead show your loved ones how much you can shine.

We can run a million miles. We can spend a hundred lifetimes chasing our tails.
We can keep moving and moving.
In the end, it is only ourselves that can find our peace.
Stop today and listen deep inside you – therein lies all your healing and peace.

Turn yourself upside-down and see things another way around!
Having the courage to do this is a great moment and life will never feel the same again. You will never feel 'tied up' again in your way of thinking.

Gold is the colour I see flowing from your hands today allowing you to shine and to be strong in the way of saying "No" to others and saying "Yes" to you.

In these moments you allow love to simply flow in and you can welcome the happiness of all that is about to enter your life.

With this energy you will begin to shine an even brighter light for others because you placed yourself first.

Trust that Spirit brings the right people to our loved ones when we are not around and they are in need of love and protection. In doing this, you can live a more enriched life without the fear and worry that they will be okay.

They are loved and, once you understand this, you then hold a greater energy to share with all those around you and those you wish to send healing to.

We cannot heal others or ourselves if we hold onto fear in anyway. The energy you feel is the energy you send to others.

Trust is your key to positive healing.

We can easily spend all our lives trying to 'fix' everything when, so often, all we ever need do is just sit and listen with a caring ear.

The beautiful power of healing is beyond our true understanding, it's beyond any words we could ever say, it's beyond any writing we could ever write but it is never beyond our reach!

Let go of any issues you may have with someone, and say, "Whatever issues we once held, today I am letting go of them all!"

You CAN do it, because you are strong and loving. Do this with an intention of sending love and not simply of letting go of anger. In this way everyone wins!

Watch how happiness will return, not just to you but also to every single soul around you.

Today let us all start afresh, let us all begin
to see life's lessons in another way.
Today let us all find the positive reasons in
all the challenges that come our way!

When you start to truly accept your path, however steep the climb may feel, let go of blame.

Look up and say, "Whatever these lessons may be for, I believe all is for my higher good." Then Magic begins!

The secret lies in a deep acceptance that all is as it should be.

Take your next amazing step and just trust. Now, get ready for your miracles!

Love is a miracle which we are all born with. The mind may try to delay this miracle with issues, but the heart never stops telling you that, above all, love is who you are!

Truth sits patiently waiting for the day when we open our hearts and understand that life is simple. It is only our minds that complicate our paths.

I choose to be happy.
I choose to help.
I choose to love.
I choose to give.
I choose to listen to my heart.
I choose not to listen to my mind.
I choose not to get angry.
I choose not to hold onto the past.
I choose to believe that everything will be fine.
I choose to trust in the Universe for it is only I who can choose what life brings and how I feel.

Today is your day and your word is 'Yes'.
If anyone asks you to do something wonderful, if anyone offers you a gift, if anyone
wants to help you...remember today to
smile and say "Yes".

At times, the harder you try the more things fall apart.
If you feel this happening slow down, stop trying, keep trusting.

Today is a brand new beginning, filled with the energy of red. Red is our colour of love.

You will have a new idea which will inspire you to be successful in everyway.

You are all you need to be.

There is no such thing as death. We are all souls passing through, learning important lessons to help us become even more beautiful.

We are all here to find our way home and, along the way, we meet many souls who help us to see who we truly are and what we have come here to learn.

Remember to always be kind and caring. Always do your best. That is all that is ever asked of you.

You are the Master - never bow to anyone.
If you truly feel the need to bow to anyone, here, take my mirror!

Letting go of fear and learning to trust the heart leads us to a true place of healing. There is nothing that light and love cannot overcome.

You are made so beautiful; you are so very perfect.

You are learning so much in this life and, by letting go of all the negative thoughts in your mind, you become crystal clear with lightness like never before. You become more loving and more understanding with everyone and even more so, with yourself.

Love yourself without the feelings of selfishness or sacrifice. You are beautiful and you deserve to have your time and space.

In doing this you become a higher energy; a new energy that then heals every situation within and around you.

Smile at least once a day to someone you have never seen before.
You just never know, your smile may have just saved their heart!

Just because you may have never seen an angel, does not mean they don't exist. The one thing that will never be spoiled by mankind is proof that there is a spirit world.

We are all here to learn the greatest lesson of all - Faith.

Be happy when you see love around you and like magic, love comes.

Be joyful for others when good things happen for them and watch how joy will flow into your life.

Give with all your heart and your heart will always receive in return.

Take a little time today for you and for your healing.

Sit in a quiet place and just be. Allow any thoughts into your mind. Allow them to stay if they want to or, if they decide to leave, simply let them go.

The secret to meditation is not to fight with the mind but to breathe deeply, smile and repeat, "Everything is exactly as it should be". Repeating these words heals more than you could ever imagine.

Sometimes it's good to keep your thoughts to yourself though always be a shoulder ready for your loved ones to cry on.
Wisdom is not always sharing your thoughts, it is knowing when the time is right to share them.

Close your eyes. See yourself on a hot air balloon, feel the balloon lifting up into the air. Feel your heart flowing with this motion.

This is how your life can be, flowing with no sense of time.

No need to worry which way you are going for now the Universe is gently taking you on your path.

This way of life you are already working towards - start your journey today and float, feeling the lightness and trust.

Start a small monthly get-together and focus on sending healing to one person. See what happens. Soon you will be healing many.

Take time this day to go through some old photos of you and your loved ones and those you love and miss in Spirit.

Choose the ones that touch your heart deeply as you look at them.

Put all these photos together in a large mounting so that your heart will smile each day as you catch a glimpse of this creation of loving memories.

Do this for Spirit; do this for you.

There is a beautiful aura around you today. Deep within your aura shines the colour purple.

You are so blessed as this is your sign of a deeper connection to Spirit.

Smile in the knowing of how far you have travelled in this your life to have this true connection to your guides and your loved ones in Spirit.

Even the smallest of birds has a song to sing. You too have a song. Never be afraid to sing your song.

What is important to remember is that as you do, your song will be heard by the right people.

Start each day by saying "Thank You" even though you can't know what the day might bring.

A daily practice of heart-felt gratitude is confirmation of you placing your trust in Spirit that they will not let you down and, in the end, they never will.

Take three crystals and make three journeys.

First, find a place near water – lake, river or sea. Say a prayer there for someone who is not well and then plant your crystal.

Next, journey to a place you loved as a child or that you love right now. Pray there for YOU, giving thanks for your health and life. Plant this second crystal.

The third journey will be to the highest mountain or hill. Once there, say a prayer to Spirit, to Mother Nature giving thanks for their love. Plant the third crystal.

Each day thereafter, in the morning and night, close your eyes and see each place you planted your crystals. Feel the power and love you hold to change your world around you and send healing to all who need a healing hand.

Holding onto old love means there is never quite enough room for a new true love to exist in your life. This will play heavy on the heart.

Today, say "Thank you" to your old loves and then let them go. In this moment you invite in a new energy of freedom and have made room for a new love to exist and flourish in your life.

Never spend a moment's thoughts longing for other people's gifts. Your time here is precious and your gifts are all you need to focus on. Yes, you are gifted, dear friend.

Anytime your heart speaks to you with a beautiful, uplifting message be sure to share that message, for it is not only intended for you.

This is how Spirit works through you, and this message will be seen and felt by all the right people who need it at that divine moment.

If you are looking for true love, you must begin by first discovering your inner love.

Work on letting go of past issues and focus on loving yourself.

Once we find our inner love, we create a powerful energy that touches those around us and gives us a renewed and amazing love for life.

Your inner love begins when you believe in your own self-worth and value.

At times what we feel as anger is really frustration.

This frustration disables us from listening.

Unable to listen, we can miss all the signs being provided to us.

In these moments, we can so easily make mistakes.

Go gently. Take care with your actions and let go of anger and frustration.

Be open and prepared for what may come your way today and the greatest opportunities Spirit has planned for you.

Breathe in through your nose and out through your mouth.
Breathe in and feel the love of life.
Breathe out and release all of your worries and fears.

The father figure is all around you today, sending you his heart and protection.
Today I just wanted you to know that your father loves you and always has.
Please say hello to your father today and make his day.

Deep inside you there is a strength so powerful you can alter your world in any given moment.
Today, take your leap of faith, look up and say! "Ok, here I go! If I fall, I know you will catch me!"

I hug my daughter, I hug my cat, I hug my dogs, I hug my wife, I hug my friends, I hug strangers, I hug boxes of chocolates, I hug trees...what have YOU hugged lately?

Happiness
U
Give

Beautiful souls who make the most effort to heal themselves and see their inner flames are the ones that magic always comes to much quicker.

Spirit loves to see you believe and always has a helping hand ready and waiting for the moment you find your inner faith, in you.

Once we realise that there is no separation between nature and ourselves, we then start to heal our world.

And in healing our world, we heal ourselves.

We are all connected to our Mother Earth and awakening to this connection is part of our destiny.

The best holiday you can give yourself is a holiday from your mind. Book today!

Allow Mother Nature to be your teacher,
allow synchronicity to be your guide.

In times of darkness, seek your truth within your heart.

What does it tell you? What do you truly feel?

Clear your fears by not allowing your mind to cloud your truth. If you allow your mind to work in these moments it creates nothing other than confusion.

Your heart is the key to your healing and it is your purest connection to all the whispers from your loved ones in Spirit. Allow yourself to feel and hear their truth.

Remember that all is as it should be and, in the end, we will know why these moments of darkness entered our lives.

Stay strong and allow life to flow from your beautiful heart. You can overcome the darkness when you seek your light.

You are a very old soul.
You are a great poet and your writing is so beautiful.
Begin today and write your book and heal with each page.
Recall all the amazing miracles and challenges you have faced and conquered in this, your book of life.
Get started and enjoy the thoughts that make you who you are.

The greatest battle is between the heart and mind.
A great start to winning this battle is by simply not allowing your mind to shout louder than your heart.

When we truly learn forgiveness, the world will be healed.

Never accept or excuse the wrong doings or violent actions of anyone. But, in saying "I forgive you, not your actions", you begin to release your pain and continue the flow to your beautiful life. Never give up on your own power of forgiveness.

This day is a beautiful one as it is a day of re-awakening. Get ready for your magic!

There are times we must trust in a power
that is beyond our understanding.

Never cry another person's tears. The only way to healing the pain of our loved ones is to understand that we all have our tests to conquer.

Always believe in your loved ones. Don't create fear or doubt their ability to conquer the tests that come their way.

Today, smile at your loved ones and tell them: "I love you and know you can do this!"

Black is a beautiful colour and it speaks in a powerful way about you today.

Fear not the colour black, for around you it signifies that something quite amazing you have been long awaiting is just about here.

You will soon know what this is and, at the very moment you do, smile and remember that this is a moment of change. Your world will soon be flooded with many colours and you will shine even brighter inside and out.

Each time you fall and pick yourself back up you will be there for someone who has fallen where you once lay. Our moments of pain serve us in helping others to heal faster through our deeper understanding of their pain.

There is no darkness that can take your light. Repeat after me, "No one has the power over me."

Today is a beautiful day to simply look up and say: "For the next seven days, I will get up, make my breakfast, get on with my day and get into bed but with one commitment - I will do this without carrying around worry or fear over what might happen or go wrong in these seven days."

Be your light and let the world see how bright you shine.
When others see that all you ever need is to keep that light shining bright, they soon will follow the way of their light.

You are stronger than you could ever imagine.
You are brighter than ever before.
You shine bright and your energy is of yellow. Yellow like that of a lion, ready to see and to conquer all.
Your mind is clear and ready for a new beginning.

Each step you make, each breath you take brings you one step closer to the top of your mountain.

At times you may slip as the mountain you choose is a steep one - the most powerful souls choose the steepest of mountains.

Once you reach the top you will take that first deep breath and look across the world and know that it was you and only you who conquered your mountain!

Keep on climbing, you are a beautiful, strong soul.

Love comes not when we pray for love but when we work on loving ourselves.
The more we love ourselves, the more love comes our way.

Believe in your signs - they are all around you!

Spirit is with you today, shining a brilliant light around you.

Your family, in Spirit, would like you to know how much they love you. They are smiling and love to watch you shine with happiness.

When you are feeling sad, they too feel sad with you.

So please, if there was ever a good reason to find your happiness, it would be that your joy brings your loved ones in Spirit the greatest of happiness.

Today is a beautiful day to stand still
A lighthouse does not have any need to move yet it brings comfort to all who see its light shine.
This is who you are, never doubt this and shine in your light.

In the natural flow of life a flower will lose its beautiful petals. In doing so, that flower becomes even more beautiful, ready for new life. Like the flower, let go and watch your life renew into the most amazing flower that life could bring.

Today make a simple promise. If you find yourself judging anyone, stop! Slap your wrist and say sorry to your heart.

Trust, believe and give thanks for all that you are about to receive.

The last part in your understanding will be when you realise that YOU are the missing piece of your happiness and path.
You, my wonderful friend, are the teacher. In time you will understand this. I see it and know that great wisdom exists in you.

You are filled with a calming pink energy today, it's so beautiful and tells me who you are and where you are going.

You are filled with love and empathy for all who walk into your life. With strength to accept life's challenges, this new energy is given to you as a gift today, to help you help others which in turn helps your true purpose in life.

Today may just be that day which opens your heart to see and confirm why you are here, open your heart and listen.

Your heart wants to be free.
Do not allow anyone to steal your power
or to overshadow your light.
Today, fly like you have never flown before
and Spirit will always keep you safe.

The most powerful act you can do for your happiness is to simply allow life to flow and synchronicity to play its part in your life.

Clear your mind and listen to your heart. Conquer this, and there are no limits to what your heart believes you can and always have been able to do!

As I walk my path I hear words with each step I take; trust, believe, smile, love, heal, happiness.

Each step I take is filled with the joys of strength, that knowing, in the end, everything will be fine; all because I trust and listen with all my heart.

Spirit has a divine plan for us all that is exactly as is should be.

Today, focus on all the blessings you were ever given and give thanks for all you are about to receive.

Feel this gratitude inside you.

This energy will grow within your heart and Spirit takes notice. How can Spirit give us what we deserve when we don't say thank you for all we have received?

Today, start to think and feel all the gifts you hold inside you, think and feel all the love and blessings you have been given.

Look up and say "Thank You".

We all have days when life feels like a web of tangled emotions and finding a way to solve all our issues can be overwhelming. In such a moment, take time to still yourself or go into nature and start to resolve these issues by simply taking one issue at a time. Feel it and then send it up to Spirit to handle.

From that moment, do not dwell on this issue again, just trust that it will resolve in its perfect time.

You will soon understand that your issues are never yours to handle alone.

Spirit watches and is always working to help you.

I see within you the deep colour of green. This tells me that you are on a beautiful path of healing, inside and out.

Today feel good about yourself, as Spirit confirms that you are growing stronger. Peace is entering your life bringing you all the healing you ever wished for.

Right at this moment, right where you are, know that you are healing more than ever. Smile and be happy. Your body is a temple, and what you put into it and how you look after it is as much healing and as important as any other action you take today.

You are your healing.

Today is a beautiful day to show your love and appreciation to Spirit and to the world. Go and shake the hands of as many people as possible today – share your happiness through these healing handshakes.

You have an amazing motherly instinct, a caring way with children.

You are an angel in many ways. Never doubt how amazing you are.

The children who have had the gift of your love are the luckiest children for their foundations are strong.

The time and love you devoted to them have become the strong foundations on which they now build a happy life.

Be proud of who you are and how beautiful you are to your loved ones.

Today, take time to meditate for you see so much more when you close your eyes.
You are creative and shine a light so bright into this world.
Today, I want you to know that you are needed here right now.
Go shine your beautiful light!

Spirit knows that you have asked for help.
Today say "Thank You" because they are
helping you as far as your path allows.
Work with them and trust that all is about
to shine.

When someone is in complete darkness they may find it difficult to see that spiritual light for the first time. If they ask for light, we must slowly open that door and allow them time to grow in the love of that spiritual light. Remember to always keep that door open for as and when they are ready.

If we always work towards recognising our actions and reactions we will always grow spiritually and become one with ourselves to fill the world with love and light

I smile because I am smiling inside.
I love because I feel love inside.
I am kind because I care.
I am caring because I am sensitive.
I spread kindness because I know it is the only thing the Universe is asking of me right now.
Be the light and show the world how kind you can be.

Magic lies in planting seeds of happiness along our path. The secret is not to stop and watch them grow, rather it is to keep on planting.

Never give up on anyone, because to do so is like giving up on yourself.

As you feel the pain through the loss of a loved one, consider if you might never have had the chance to love that very soul who loved you back, to be free from the pain you hold within you.

Take heart and allow your pain to ease. Soon you will rejoice in each single day you shared with the souls you have loved and you will acknowledge those moments are worth all the pain you have suffered.

There are no limits to your amazing life. There is no one who ever wants to stop you. There is no one who does not believe in you, there is no one who is ever angry with you, there is no one who hates you and there is no one who thinks you're a failure.

Those who may cause you to feel this way are merely showing their own fear and anger. Deep in their hearts they wish they could do all that you are about to do. You are amazing and you are about to change your life.

This moment is yours and I am here to tell you, "YOU CAN DO IT!"

Now lift yourself up and spread your wings, for the world is waiting!

We are all here for one another.

At times when we feel down, as though life is getting a little too much, trust that beyond your mind is another world; a world that works constantly to help you through your harder moments.

Like a miracle to us, someone walks into your life to help you back up.

If there is a time that you may fall down and it feels as if no one is around, that is when this miracle happens.

Our journey is one of many emotions.
To be comfortable with our sad days, to accept those days and just flow with them without trying to find a reason 'why?' is equal to accepting all of our wonderful happy days.

Send love to those who you feel would never deserve it; they do - more than we know.

To send pure healing there can be no boundaries.

A pure heart is, therefore, the most powerful healer of all.

The best gift we can ever receive is happiness; the best gift we can ever give is happiness.

Healing is a gift from Spirit that relights your inner flame.

The power of Spirit's gift is the most amazing love we could ever receive in our hearts.

Ask Spirit for a helping hand each and every day.

Live your beautiful life without the fear and worry that those you love will be ok.
It is not possible to heal if we hold on to fear in anyway and so it is true in wanting to heal others. The energy you feel is the energy you send to others.
Trust is your key to an even greater energy, which in turn heals the ones we love.

There is a new vibration in our Universe and people are becoming stronger. Spirit's message is being heard through the voices of so many people. More light workers are being born and re-born.

Love is spreading and this energy is bringing a new sense of hope and trust to our world. You will start to see all the world repairing and more people are seeing miracles each and everyday.

Walk and listen with your heart, breath in Mother Nature and feel her warmth, love and protection.

Each and every one of us has a higher divine purpose which can reveal itself in many ways.
If you are yet to discover yours then never lose your faith and courage. Believe it to live it.

Shine your light. Even if you think you have made no difference, know that you have. Light works like pure water - it may take a little time but, in the end, it seeps into even the smallest of cracks. Never give up.

What holds us up, what keeps us going, what lifts us up when we fall, what gives us hope, what gives us peace, what clears the fears and worries in our everyday life?

Only we have the inner strength to clear and strengthen all the above but it starts with our faith in our 'other side'; that beautiful veil between our two world's.

Once we open our hearts we open our eyes to all the signs Spirit, our loved one's, are giving us each and every day.

So make today the reason to find your faith and clear your clouds of doubt. Trust, believe, and receive.

Synchronicity is Spirit's gift of a helping hand.

No one can hold you back; no one can hold you down.

You are someone who gets up and takes action.

Someone who loves to make things happen and loves life.

You have the power to see the light in the dark, to help many in times of trouble.

Today I thank you for being you, for being a kind soul in this world.

Never change for you are just who you need to be.

The walls you build around you, that you feel are needed to protect your heart from hurting, will soon be exchanged for a new energy.

Feel and embrace this new energy, look up and say:

"Today I will open up and trust that you, my amazing family in Spirit, will now bring all the right people into my life. I will learn to see that the most powerful energy is not trying to protect myself rather it is in being open to receiving the love and magic now on its way into my life."

Sometimes it seems as though we have it all, and yet we feel as if we walk our path alone.

This, dear friend, is a great blessing and not one to feel sad about.

You are special and unique. Stand strong; make a difference in this world.

Be a leader and a light for others who may be in darkness.

Today love is around you, in loving hands and caring hearts.

Spirit holds you in her wings. Her whispers are clearing away your very worry.

Today your life will be filled with smiles and love.

This is your moment. Go out and allow yourself the gift of love for you deserve all the love in your life.

Today when you talk about others, do it in a way that focuses only on all that is amazing about them.

Today, cut the cords of your past by simply placing your hand on your stomach and saying these words: "What was once, is no longer - I unlock my chains and free my soul, clear my cords and allow myself to simply fly free."

Always do your best to help people, but take care not to step over the line between helping and living someone else's life. Otherwise you may learn a very hard lesson.

It's your moment to put on bright and beautiful clothes, to show the world you are not afraid to be different, to show the world how strong and happy you are.

From today, never again be afraid to stand out in a crowd. This is your moment - shine and allow people to love you for who you are.

Entering into conflict serves no purpose in your happiness.

Don't spend your time judging others or being a part of other people's weaknesses.

Work lovingly towards peace in your life and do not allow anyone to pull you down to a lower vibration of living.

Remember there is nothing more powerful than working on your own happiness.

You deserve all the magic in our world.

Smile and get ready for all that Spirit is about to bring to you.

Your voice is not just a voice.
Your words are not just words.
All that you are and all that you say creates
a powerful vibration.
You carry this energy within you.
It touches souls and heals many.

Looking into your eyes today, I see a tiger. One which knows and sees all the important things that will bring you closer to your happiness.

Today you will see things more clearly and, through this energy, a beautiful day will unfold.

When our clothes are dirty, what do we do? Wash them.

And so it is true that when our energy is 'dirty' we need to clean it away.

Treat yourself to a massage or a healing session. Not only because it will help you but also because you so deserve it.

If you walk in the footsteps of others, you will eventually look back over your shoulder and realise you never left your own beautiful mark in this life.
Take your own steps and never be afraid to take leaps of faith!

Life takes the strong to places they didn't even know they could conquer.

Your mind will always try to limit the possibilities that are within your life's journey. Open your mind and allow all your dreams to come flooding in.
Your dreams are only just a step away from reality - start living your dreams today.

Placing trust in Spirit and asking for a little help from Spirit is a beautiful thing to do. Your trust enables you to work together with Spirit and to help others in the world.

You are beautiful, you are amazing, you are filled with love, your heart is so bright and strong, your life is magical, miracles are happening right in front of you as you read this.

Flow with life, without conflict, judgment, anger, worry and fear.

Today look up and simply say, "You look after all my issues and I'll just enjoy this day You have given me!"

Don't remain focused on the negative energy from another. Rise above this draining energy.

Lessons will make us stronger as long as we recognize them and then let them go.

Focus on spreading your own light – shine!

Remember you are loved and protected.

Choose to see the light in everyone today.

"Everything is as it should be." Repeat this every time you need to know the time.

Are you someone who spends your life chasing your tail? Today STOP! Be instead like the wise owl that sits still, patiently knowing everything will come to her in good time.

You are wonderful.
You have the ability to give.
You are devoted.
You are loving towards your family and your heart is like a beautiful rose.
You always have a caring ear and an understanding soul.
You are not judgmental.
You, amazing friend, are simply perfect today!

At times we carry around so many issues that they feel like such a weight on our shoulders.

Today, let go of any issues. Step back. Go for a short journey away from where you live.

Step out of this bubble you have found yourself in.

Allow yourself to look inside that bubble, the one that keeps you frozen.

Then, you might just find the answers.

It is a beautiful feeling to know that some-one cares about us and sees us as beautiful. Be happy today in the knowing that you HAVE many caring eyes watching over you, in this world and in our beautiful Spirit world.

There is a beautiful new place I have just found. I wanted to share it with all my friends as soon as I got there, for it has filled me with all the feelings we so need in life, those feelings that calm us all down when we get so stressed and worried.

It only takes a little time and practice to get there. You would truly love it, I know you would.

So now it is up to you. All I can do is tell you how amazing it is and where it is and how it has changed my life forever. I am at peace forever after going there. It touched me so deeply that I really never knew a place could ever do this to anyone. Today I wanted you all to know where it is.

The place I went to was, my heart!

To find peace of mind we need to master the arts of patience and forgiveness.

Do not fill your days with worry. Let go and trust that things will all be well in time.

Do not hold onto anger or be weighed down by this destructive emotion.

Work on you and work towards finding happiness within you - for no matter how long you search, you will not find your happiness through anyone else.

You, and you alone, will be the master of your happiness.

To have many conflicts in life does not mean we are cursed. It simply means we are strong enough to conquer all our challenges.

Today, write a poem and gift it to the world. Magic comes from the heart and it is the place from where all poetry flows.

Orange is the colour I see surround you today. The colour of a burning desire, a desire to be strong, to feel free and to follow your intuition.

Listen to what feels right inside of you now. Be kind to yourself and today it is important to put your happiness first.

The burning flame of orange is a reminder to be strong, that this is your day.

Today, this afternoon and this evening, say a prayer for the first person you think of that doesn't understand you. Be the strength of their healing. You will feel how much more beautiful it is to be this way, rather than trapped in a world of judgment.

A true healer never asked you to bow in front of them or to kiss their feet.
A true healer will tell you that we are all equal.
You don't have to sit under a tree for twenty years to receive enlightenment
All you need do is simply believe in your destiny and inner power.
You are the guru, you are the answer to everything.

Make that call to someone you love today, and tell him or her how much you care.

The way to beautiful conversation is to not have something to say until friends who are talking have finished. Give it a try.

To understand karma is simple. How people react to you is their karma and how you react back is yours. This is a great measuring stick.

For those who seek help, Spirit will find a way to lead them to the right people for help and protection.

By surrendering what you were taught,
you begin to allow Mother Nature, Spirit,
and our amazing Universe to gently whis-
per in your heart,
Listen to what comes deep from the heart,
for there wait all the answers!

All you ever need is to remember who you are. Beautifully perfect, you are everything you ever need to be. Within you is more wisdom than you could ever imagine. Your heart is so powerful, there is nothing you cannot handle.

If you could see what I see in you, there would be no mountain you could not climb, no love you could not feel and no happiness you could not achieve.

Stop focusing on the 'what ifs?'

Make this day the first day of the rest of your life. Take control of the driving wheel of your life and don't allow anyone to stop you. Don't think for a moment about what others will think, this is your life, your moment, now take that leap of faith and be who you were always meant to be – amazing.

As I walk along this path of life, I always remind myself to live with kindness, to speak words of love and to always live from the heart.

I don't allow any time to fight, to hate or to live with jealousy.

I show love and see the best in everyone – if you shine, I shine; if you smile, I smile; if you tell me you care, I will always love you.

Your task for today is to close your eyes, feel with your heart and write down your own healing quote. Share these beautiful words for others to feel and be healed.

The real secret of why we are here is to be open. To know that our most painful paths can be the greatest goals for our higher understanding, allowing us to reach a new and higher vibration.

Remember, we see the light best when in the darkness.

Spirit has heard your wish. When the moment is divine, your wish will become part of your life.
All you now need do is just simply get on with your beautiful journey.

This week, give yourself a rest from all newspapers and TV. Focus this time instead on something or someone you love. This indeed is a wonderful exchange.

When you open your heart and world to Spirit, it will move mountains.

Tears are the sign of a heart opening.

Today is a good day to watch your step.
Keep your eyes on the road and listen to
your heart.
It always knows things before they happen.
If your heart feels there could be big waves
ahead, trust those feelings.
You know, you always know.

We all lose faith sometimes.
This too is part of our journey to self-discovery.
But faith never dies in the heart and soul.
Re-awaken your flame and live life as you were always meant to: in love, in peace and in balance.

Stop for a moment and look back over the past few years. Despite challenging times you may have been through and painful memories, you are still here.

Now imagine if you had always known that you would be fine today and that all you have been through would bring you to right here and now. Can you imagine all the hours of worry you could have lived without? So tell me, knowing this now how are you going to live your life from today?

Ask yourself why your challenges have made you who you are today, and see how they made you stronger. This is indeed the most amazing healing you could give yourself.

Today is a beautiful day to listen to music. It will feed your soul with a great energy and fill your heart with joy.

The warrior in you has awakened. This part of your journey is to stand strong and to not give up.

Who is the first person that springs to mind when you hear the word 'beautiful'? If your answer is anything other than YOU, then you still haven't grasped the full beauty within you. Keep trying! Here, grab this mirror; it will help to remind you how amazing you are.

Today let us pray for the entire world, and for our brothers and sisters who are going through challenges we could not imagine. Ask your loved ones in Spirit to help heal their burden and bring a little light into their world today.

We do not truly own anything in our lifetime, we simply borrow it for the time we are here. Our love is what is ours to give away freely, and it is wonderful when we can pass our love onto our children. They, in turn will pass this love onto their children. Love, unlike possessions, lasts forever and is never forgotten.

When you believe in someone, share your belief with them today. You will bring an energy into their life that may just help them become the greatest soul they could ever dream to be.

Close your eyes and think of the first colour that comes to you. Embrace this
colour and then find a way to bring this
colour into your life.

To be kind, to be caring, to be beautiful.
To be honest, to be loyal, to be loving.
This is all you ever need be and – you are!

Your task for today is to simply skip! Yes, just like you did as a child!

The heart that gives is always full.

A gift should always be given without holding onto its value. If you do hold onto its value, it was never a gift to begin with.

Your task for today is to simply laugh! Why wait for it to happen? Go on, do it now!

Always remember to place your most loving energy into even the smallest of actions for others today. By being and doing your best in everything, shows others who you truly are.

Often our greatest heroes are the ones who feel pain the most, battle the most, and live the hardest of challenges. The stronger we are the more we go through in life.

Listen to what others are saying, and always remember that what they say is what they too have to learn and conquer.

The quickest way to dispel anger is through a smile.

A heart that is open is a heart that heals most.

There are people that will take a simple solution and make it into something more complicated. True answers are the simplest ones. Take the time to listen and you will find the answer in simplicity.

Never underestimate the power of your dreams. One day, you may look back and realise that everything you dreamed of came true.

This is my path. I trust in each step that I take from this day forward. This is my moment to shine.

Hold your Thoughts – Healing Page

This space is dedicated to those that may be in need of a little healing (you may like to add a name of a person, a pet, a country that you wish to dedicate some healing time to)

Hold your Thoughts – Personal Inspiration

Add to this book and create your own healing thoughts, we all have the power within to heal ourselves and the world we live in.

Hold your Thoughts – Poetry

Allow the words to simply flow from your heart. They don't need to rhyme to touch the hearts of others.

Hold your Thoughts – Your Dreams

Your dreams are just a step away - write down some of your dreams and keep them in your daily sights!

In the stillness we find the answers.

10412601R00108

Printed in Great Britai
by Amazon.co.uk, Ltd
Marston Gate.

the
WARREN SMITH SKI ACADEMY
is sponsored by:

swiss.com

volkl.com

oakley.com

sidas.com

dainese.com

mammut.ch

scottusa.com

the
ACADEMY HANDBOOK
is produced in association with:

SAASTAL

BERGBAHNEN

WARREN SMITH - PROFILE

Warren Smith is one of Britain's leading professional freeskiers and an Internationally Certified Performance Coach. He has spent many years teaching recreational skiers, developing ski instructors and coaching racers all over Europe. He is one of the most innovative instructors working in the Alps today and has earned a name for himself for getting results for his students.

Warren is a member of the International Ski Instructors Association, a member of the International Ski Coaching Federation, a UK Snowsports Coach & Tutor, a British Free-skiing Competitor, a producer and presenter of the highly acclaimed tuition video series 'The Ultimate Learning Experience' and a Presenter of cable TV's 'Ski Tips', and holds a Diploma in 'Sports Psychology'.

Warren Smith Profile
www.soulsports.co.uk/warrensmith

CONTENTS

Introduction

CONTENTS

THE HANDBOOKS

The Warren Smith Ski Academy has been changing and developing skiers' technique for over a decade. It has earned a reputation for getting results for people who are at the intermediate, advanced and expert levels of skiing.

The Warren Smith Ski Academy Handbooks were compiled after hundreds of requests from people who bought the Warren Smith Ski Academy DVDs. The Handbooks follow the same format as the DVDs - using the same headings and explanatory images - and so are the perfect compliment to the DVDs, putting down in writing what you see on the screen. The Handbooks fit conveniently into your pocket and you can browse them while you are on a chairlift or in the office lift.

Handbook 2 accompanies the Lesson 2 DVD - and follows on from Handbook 1 with technique solutions for further progression with Carving, Steeps, Moguls and Freeride. As with Handbook 1, it is divided into four chapters, with one chapter for each discipline. Each chapter is a mixture of Theory, Exercises and Images, divided into four key elements. At the beginning of each element you will find a column which has been left blank for your own notes and thoughts.

Theory, Exercises & Images

The Theory
You will find an explanation of the theory behind each technique.

The Exercises
The Exercises explain where and how to apply the Theory to your own technique, with tips and examples to practise on the mountain.

The Images
Give you a visual understanding of where you might be going wrong and what you are trying to achieve.

These three things combined will help you develop your skill and build your confidence to ultimately give you a sound skiing technique.

CARVING

2

INTRODUCTION TO CARVING

Handbook 1 introduced you to the aim of carving - to travel in each direction while spending the majority of the time on the edges of your skis, with the skis cutting into and carving arcs through the snow. If you have practised the tips, examples and exercises outlined in Handbook 1 you should better understand this aim by now.

This chapter focuses on the ways in which you can push your carving technique to the next level - with further tips, examples and exercises to help you progress.

SPEED TRAINING

CONTROLLING BODY ROTATION

ONE LEGGED SKIING

LEFT AND RIGHT TURN DIFFERENCES

CARVING

A
SPEED TRAINING

As your carving technique develops and improves, you will feel able to increase the speed of the movement at which you travel across the snow and from edge to edge.

SPEED STANCE

When you start to increase your carving speed it is important to be aware of how to make your body react better when you start to take corners faster. Here it is quite useful to compare the technique used to carve a turn to the techniques used for other sports that also require good control and dynamics for going around corners at higher speeds (**fig. 1**).

fig. 1 - fast cornering

Take cars as an example. To better handle the speed of a fast car, you would choose a wheel and tyre that are wider in dimension and lower to the ground (**fig. 2**).

fig. 2 - a wide and low tyre for a fast car

Similar adjustments should be made to width and height when choosing the best position for skiing at speed.

The stance that is best suited for faster skiing is slightly wider and more open (**fig. 3**) as it gives you a more stable platform. You should also adopt a position that is lower to the ground, as this lowers your centre of gravity (**fig. 4**). In addition you should make the appropriate adjustments to the upper body.

fig. 3 - a wider and more open stance

fig. 4 - get low

These changes might feel subtle, but the difference the combination of a wider and more open stance and a lower position makes is very noticeable when you increase the speed at which you ski. When you adjust your stance and position in this way you need to follow a few pointers to make sure you are making the right kind of changes.

CARVING

Width Adjustments

A common problem among skiers when they begin to ski faster is that, instinctively, they only open out their stance from the feet. This leaves their knees closer together than their frame, in an 'A-Frame' shape (**fig. 5**). This position causes the skis to lean at different angles. When you widen your stance it is essential to ensure that you open out your knees and your feet, not just your feet on their own.

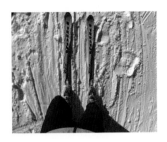

fig. 6 - knees and feet check

fig. 5 - an 'A-frame' = different edge angles

To make sure that you are not adopting an A-Frame position, check your stance while you are still in a static position (**fig. 6**). Look down your body to your knees and feet to check that you have widened your stance by moving both of these body parts out.

Height Adjustments

When you lower your position, to lower your centre of gravity, focus on shrugging your shoulders forwards, lowering your hands and flexing your ankles (**fig. 7**). This will give you a more dynamic stance, which will help you to react better when you are skiing at a higher

fig. 7 - shoulders... hands... ankles...

speed. As you flex, always make sure that you test the position of your hips - they should be driving down over the balls of your feet (**fig. 8**).

fig. 8 - hips over the balls of your feet

False Dynamics
Skiers can be fooled into thinking they have attained a dynamic stance, when actually they are just moving their weight too far forwards or too far backwards.

Many skiers, when reacting to an increase in speed, think that they are flexing all the relevant joints more when in reality they are just bending at the knees and the waist. This is a common problem, because it is easier to flex the knee joint than it is to flex the ankle joint. However the result is that the

skier's weight moves from over the balls of the feet and the skier just ends up sitting back (**fig. 9**).

fig. 9 - don't take a seat

Although this may feel like a lower and more dynamic position, as your weight is too far back it is actually very vulnerable and weak. Some skiers do the opposite - and move their weight forward (**fig. 10**).

fig. 10 - weight too far forward

Again this does not result in a lower and more dynamic position because they are not leaning their legs enough laterally. Usually they compensate for this lack of lean by squashing down their upper body and folding forward at the waist. This results in the head being the same height from the snow but in an out of balance position that creates a false dynamic and results in the skier having less control.

The key is to keep the middle of the body strong (**fig. 11**) and prevent the waist from folding over and forwards - as the waist is vulnerable to breaking or over-flexing in the same way as the knees. Therefore it needs to be supported when skiing at speed. This can be achieved by retaining

fig. 11 - retained tension = a strong middle body

a little tension in the lower stomach muscles.

STAYING IN CONTROL

As you learn to carve faster certain external factors mean you need to work harder at staying in control. These are explained using a tug-of-war analogy.

Leaning Against Forces

The first thing to do to stay in control when carving at a higher speed is to increase the lean of your legs to react against the greater forces pulling your body (**fig. 12**).

fig. 12 - higher speeds = greater forces

Imagine how you would react in your tug-of-war. You need to react to the increase of the forces pulling your body in the same way

- the more you are being pulled the more you need to lean away from the person pulling you (**fig. 13**).

fig. 14 - soften, flex
and lean

fig. 13 - greater forces =
more need to lean

As at higher speed the forces pulling you are greater you need to lean more against them. To increase your lean, allow your hips to move laterally across your skis to a greater degree when you make a turn. To help this happen you should soften, flex and lean your inside leg as you go through the turn (**fig. 14**).

Leaning To Grip
Continuing with the tug-of-war analogy, the more you are pulled around by the forces the greater grip you need to maintain with your point of contact with the surface of the snow. The harder you are

pulled in your tug of war match the more you need footwear with a good grippy sole to stick to the surface. When you ski at higher speeds you need to increase the angle of your edges more to make them grip to the snow (**fig. 15**).

fig. 15 - good edge angle

The more you lean your legs, the more the edge angle will increase.

CARVING

This will give you more of a platform to grip onto, and as you go around corners at speed, the more able you will be to exert more pressure on the snow. Ultimately both factors will give you more support. It is important to ensure two things: first that your edge angles are the same, especially at speed, and secondly that you're standing on the edges and not pushing them away.

To be sure your edge angles are the same you need to lean and steer your inside leg as much as your downhill leg. Many skiers have a lazy or unskilled inside leg (**fig. 16**). It is essential to focus more attention on the inside leg to make it more proactive and to make sure it is working to full efficiency.

fig. 16 - inactive inside leg

You must stand on the edges of the skis rather than push them away to maintain the hold that they have and to avoid a skidded carve (**fig. 17**).

pure carve

skidded carve

fig. 17 - red = pure carve, blue = skidded carve

Many skiers lack the skill, experience and confidence to maintain an edge grip throughout the whole of the turn and many find that as they go through a turn they push against the edges, moving them away from underneath the body and out to the side. This may come from being taught during earlier skiing days to "push against the downhill ski".

As you proceed to more advanced levels of skiing this needs to change so that you are standing on the skis and keeping the ski edges beneath you. This can be achieved by assuring that the pressure you put on the ski is downwards rather than outwards (**fig. 18**).

fig. 18 - downwards, not outwards pressure

DYNAMIC CROSSOVERS

Handbook 1 looked at the importance of making a dynamic crossover during the turn (**fig. 19**). This is also needed when you increase your skiing speed. It is important that there is not too much delay - or an upwards movement of the body - as you cross over from the end of one turn to the start of a new turn.

Many intermediate skiers come upwards between turns as they believe this helps to make the

fig. 19 - dynamic crossover

change from one edge to the other lighter and more easy to predict. An upwards movement like this does not cause too many problems when you are skiing at slower and less dynamic levels, but as your speed and dynamics increase the upwards movement makes the change from edge to edge too slow. When you are travelling at higher speeds the longer you spend moving upwards during the crossover the longer the skis are at a flatter angle to the slope. This results in them skidding sideways more. Also, the taller your stance in between turns the less dynamic it will be.

A more advanced way to cross over from one turn to the next is by making a 'Downhill Leg Release'.

**EXERCISE 1
RELEASING THE
PRESSURE**

THE AIM
To release the pressure and make the leaning and steering of the downhill leg more active.

WHERE
Use a gentle terrain, either a green or blue run. At this gradient the pressure build up against the downhill leg will not be so extreme and it will be easier to get the feeling.

How
As you come towards the end of one turn, start to release the pressure that is on the downhill ski so that you can roll that leg across the skis and into the new direction of the turn (**fig. 20**). You will immediately feel how this release pulls the body across the skis and tilts the skis onto the new edges (**fig. 21**).

fig. 20 - release pressure and roll leg across...

THE RESULT
The edge change of the skis from one turn to the next is lower and faster and you retain a lower stance during the crossover.

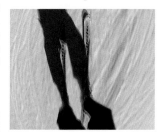

fig. 21 - ...onto the new edge

SAFETY AND EQUIPMENT

As with any sport or activity, the faster you move, the more dangerous it can become. When you start to ski faster, consider a few safety checks to reduce the chance of injury to yourself and others skiing near you.

Awareness

Try to be aware of where and on what you are skiing. At higher speeds there is less time to react to other skiers and to changes in the terrain. A good knowledge of the type of terrain, its gradient, the width and length of the slopes and the general snow conditions will help keep you skiing safely.

Also be aware of the other skiers around you. At higher speeds there is much less time to react when you are overtaking another skier, especially if they suddenly change direction or fall over in front of you. Give yourself plenty of space and ski away from other skiers.

Equipment

If you fall at higher speeds you will meet the surface with a greater impact. You should definitely wear a crash helmet and consider wearing protective clothing (**fig. 22**) to avoid back injury and impact on your joints. Wearing these items can also protect you if others skiing faster than you happen to make a mistake and collide with you.

fig. 22 - example equipment

B
CONTROLLING BODY ROTATION

WHY SKIERS ROTATE

Many skiers, at all levels from beginner to expert, rotate a part of their body while they are skiing - be it their hips, shoulders or arms. Any rotation of these parts of the body does not help skiers to turn and can also cause them to lose their balance.

There are several reasons why skiers rotate their bodies:

- some skiers rotate because they lack the leverage in their legs to steer their skis, particularly during the early stages of learning to ski. This is usually due to poor flex in the ankle joint. Skiers who do not optimise the flex in the ankles to help them turn then look elsewhere for the power to steer the skis - normally, and misguidedly, to the hips, shoulders and arms (**fig. 23**). Handbook 1 contains tips and suggestions for improving the flex of the ankle.

**fig. 23 - power from hips,
shoulders and arms**

- some skiers rotate their body
because of the nature of skiing. It
is easy to feel nervous when you
are standing on a slippery hill and
the instinct of most skiers is to turn
the upper body into the hill (**fig. 24**).

in body rotation. This increase in
speed causes an increase in the
forces trying to pull your body out of
the turn and can lead to rotation of
the hips, shoulders or arms.

Rotating any part of your upper
body when you ski puts you in a
weaker position to react against
the forces pulling you around and
about in the turn. It can also cause
the angle of the ski edges to flatten
against the snow and this can
result in mistakes being made. For
example, if the arms move around
while you are skiing it can cause
your shoulders to rotate, which in
turn can lead to hip rotation (**fig. 25**).

**fig. 24 - upper body into
the hill**

- an increase in the speed at which
skiers are moving can also result

**fig. 25 - swinging arms
cause shoulder rotation**

A few exercises can help to reduce
or avoid these types of rotation.

**EXERCISE 2
HANDS ON HIPS**

THE AIM
To reduce hip rotation and maintain a better edge angle and a stronger edge grip.

WHERE

Use a gentle, progressive terrain, similar to that of a green or blue run. A shallow gradient will allow you to focus wholly on the exercise and not have to worry about controlling your speed so much.

How

Start by discarding your poles. Then make a turn in one direction only. As you go into the turn place your hand on the hip that is on the outside of the turn and apply pressure with your hand to push the hip inwards and slightly back (**fig. 26**). This will teach the hip to counteract the rotation.

The most essential element of this exercise is the timing (**fig. 27**). Make sure you start to apply the pressure against the hip with the hand before you do anything else in the turn.

**fig. 26 - hand on
outside hip**

**fig. 27 - progressive
movement**

The movement in the turn, from the start to the finish, needs to be progressive. The build-up of pressure must be continual - don't just push against the hip once. Once you have attempted this exercise a few times in each direction start linking the turns together. Eventually, when you feel comfortable with the counter-rotation of the hip, take the poles back and try to get the same feeling during the turn.

fig. 28 - stronger edge angle and edge grip

THE RESULT

Less rotation in your hips, a better edge angle and a stronger edge grip (fig. 28) will give you more control and more steering power in the turn.

CARVING

**EXERCISE 3
UPPER BODY
MANAGEMENT**

**THE AIM
To prevent rotation
of the upper body,
particularly the
shoulders.**

WHERE
Practice on a green or blue run to begin with.

How
First make a 'window' with your ski poles by holding them upright in front of you (**fig. 29**). Once you have your 'window', make a turn in one direction only. As you ski downhill and make the turn, concentrate on keeping the shoulders facing towards the poles, and the poles facing towards the outside of the turn. You are trying to ensure that only the legs rotate, so that the shoulders and hips face towards to the poles (**fig. 30**). If the upper body and shoulders are allowed to rotate, the skis are flattened which gives you less control (**fig. 31**).

When you have practised the exercise in both directions and feel

fig. 29 - make a 'window'

fig. 30 - only the legs rotate

comfortable with it, start linking the turns together. Make sure that you get the 'window' ready in time for the new turn.

THE RESULT
A stronger upper body position, in which the shoulders are less able to turn and the skis are less likely to flatten.

fig. 31 - the skis flatten less

ARMS AND HANDS

Arms and hands can also suffer from problems of rotation for three main reasons.

Knock On Effect
The first is the knock on effect from rotation of the hips and shoulders. The same momentum can cause the arms to swing and rotate (**fig. 32**).

fig. 32 - arms rotate due to momentum

The exercises on the previous pages that deal with hip and shoulder rotation should also solve this knock on effect.

Hands Inside Elbows
The second reason is that arms are vulnerable to rotation because of how they are placed. The speed

you travel at when you ski can cause the arms, when they are out to the side of your body, to be easily pushed back by the wind hitting the body (**fig. 33**).

fig. 33 - arms too wide

You can imagine what this feels like by visualising what would happen if you put your arm out of the window of a moving car - as soon as the wind hits the arm it is forced back. The faster you drive, the more forcefully the arm gets pushed back. The same is true with skiing. For this reason it is important to manage the way you hold your arms when you ski.

Adopt a position where the hands are slightly inside the elbows in a line down from your shoulder to your hand (**fig. 34**) - with this

fig. 34 - hands inside elbows

posture your arms are most able to react to the forces put on them. In this posture the forearm is much more solid and less likely to be pushed around.

Dropping The Hand
The third reason arms and hands can rotate is because of the way the body leans laterally when it goes through the turn. This is seen in many skiers - when they turn, the tendency is to drop the inside hand into the hill.

The exercises on the following pages will help you to develop the ideal posture and prevent the hand from dropping into the hill.

CARVING

**EXERCISE 4
HANDS INSIDE
ELBOWS**

THE AIM
**To find the ideal
position for hands
and arms.**

WHERE

Practice on a terrain on which you feel confident so you can focus on your arms.

How

Take hold of a pole and position your hands on it so that they are just inside the elbows (**fig. 35**). This will help you to see and feel the ideal position. Ski a short distance holding the pole and get used to how the arms feel in this position. Then try the same exercise, but without the pole, and repeat the movement until you feel your hands and elbows remain in the ideal position.

**fig. 35 - hands positioned
on the pole**

THE RESULT

Your arms will not be so easily pushed out from your body and consequently your skiing will feel more solid, especially at higher speeds.

**EXERCISE 5
DROPPING THE HAND**

THE AIM
To stop the inside
hand from dropping
down into the hill.

WHERE

Practice on an almost flat terrain that does not generate too much force, which might throw the arms around.

How

Rest the pole in front of you on top of your hands and then balance the pole on your hands as you ski down (**fig. 36**). You will only be able to do this if you keep your hands horizontal - if the inside hand drops into the hill the pole will slide off. Practise this exercise several times until the pole rests on your hands very securely. Then try without the pole and see if you can keep the hands horizontal.

fig. 36 - hands horizontal

THE RESULT

The inside hand does not drop down into the hill during a turn, and you can increase your speed without the arms and hands rotating.

Hands in Vision

A good rule of thumb to keep in mind when you are working on your posture and managing the rotation of the arms is to keep your hands just within your vision. If you stand and look straight ahead of you in the same way as you would when you ski you should be able to see your hands and poles in your peripheral vision (**fig. 37**). You will not be looking straight at your hands and poles but you will be able to see them from the corners of your eyes.

fig. 37 - hands and poles inside vision

If your poles drop behind or down they will go out of your vision (**fig. 38**). To work out the extent of your vision, try dropping your poles down or behind you while you are standing on the spot. Then try doing the same whilst you are skiing. In both cases you should notice that you can see your poles from the corners of your eyes. Keeping your poles within your peripheral vision is a very useful and effective way of making sure that your arms are in the most effective position for pole planting, which will help you to balance and stop your arms from rotating.

fig. 38 - out of vision

C

LEFT AND RIGHT TURN DIFFERENCES

WHAT ARE THEY?

Every skier favours turning in one direction more than the other. It is not always immediately obvious which direction is favoured, and the more advanced the skier becomes, the less it is apparent.

Skiers usually favour turning one way more than the other because one side of the brain is dominant. As a result it is not uncommon for people generally to favour one side of the body to the other or do things better with one side. Take tennis as an example - many people will choose to hold the racquet in one hand over the other and prefer serving to one side of the court than the other - and this is not necessarily dictated by whether they are left or right handed.

The same is true with skiing: which side you favour does not necessarily depend on whether you are right or left handed, or right or left footed. It is more to do with which direction the body favours when steering or falling into a turn. Which side you favour will have started right back at your first snowplough turn and usually stays with you as your skiing develops to more advanced and sometimes even expert levels.

FINDING THE WEAKER DIRECTION

You may already know which is your weaker direction. If not, you can work it out by making a series of turns down the hill - while doing so try to be more aware of what you feel as you cross over from one turn to the next. You should find that your turn in one direction feels a little more intimidating than in the other.

Checking System

It is possible to use a checking system to find out quickly which is your weaker direction. When you turn in one direction the movement will simply flow (**fig. 39**) and you will fall into the turn naturally. In the other direction the turn will feel

more blocked (**fig. 40**). The blocks are both physical and mental and are totally related to each other.

**fig. 39 - a flowing turn
with no blocks**

hip
rotation

hip
angulation

**fig. 40 - the middle body
is blocked in the image
on the left**

Blocks that you may notice include:

- the inside leg not moving across, and blocking the hip (**fig. 41**);

fig. 41 - the inside leg blocks the hip

- the hips locking and causing the whole body to rotate the skis (**fig. 42**); and

fig. 42 - hips are locked, causing the whole body to rotate the skis

- a leaning and tipping of the upper body to the inside of the turn (**fig. 43**).

fig. 43 - the upper body leans and tips

You can take a number of steps to identify these blocks:

- first put your hands on your knees and feel which inside leg it is more difficult to roll across the skis when you initiate a turn.
- then put your hands on the sides of your hips and feel which side of the body it is more difficult to push across during the early stage of the turn. Normally skiers find that the side of the body that it is more difficult to push across is on the same side as the inside leg in which they have have less movement.
- finally when you are turning check which hand or shoulder drops down into the hill and into the

inside of the turn more. You can work this out by using your vision to check whether the distance between your hands remains horizontal while you turn - or whether one hand dips down on one side (**fig. 44**).

fig. 44 - compare hand levels

Once you have worked out which is your weaker direction you can train yourself to build skill and confidence in the weaker turn.

Specific Direction Development
The next step, which will help you to increase the overall level of your skiing, is to improve the skill level of your weaker direction. Up to this point, from the first day you put on skis, you will have neglected that direction and you will have favoured your stronger, more

confident side whenever you have practised skiing exercises.

To begin with, simply run through the three steps outlined to help you identify your weaker direction. Concentrate on turning in just the weaker direction. For example, while pushing your hand against your hip, turn in your weaker direction 10 times. Then try the same exercise on the stronger side, but only once. Try to be really aware of how much more confident you felt when you were turning on your stronger side. Then return to practising the exercise 10 times turning in the weaker direction.

Eventually, after time and concentrated practice you will have trained your brain to be more skilful at controlling the less confident direction, which will help you to even out the differences between your turns (**fig. 45**).

Adopt the same approach to each of the three steps until you feel you turn equally well in each direction and that your entry into the turns in both directions is confident and not restricted in any way. This won't happen straight away and

**fig. 45 - developing the
weaker direction**

you may need to put in several
hours of work, but if you are
patient and persevere you should
soon improve. A good incentive for
persevering is to remember that
you will have been turning in your
weaker direction about 95% of the
times that you have fallen over or
made a mistake - that statistic
makes it worth the extra practice.

D

ONE LEGGED SKIING

BALANCE DEVELOPMENT

To improve your feeling for balance it can be useful to practise skiing on just one ski. When we ski with both skis it is possible to get away with making mistakes and falling out of balance because for a split second there is the option of treading on and recovering with the other ski. Because of this security blanket it is very easy to become complacent about ensuring you ski in balance - as you know you will be able to recover by using the other ski. One legged skiing helps you to sharpen your balance awareness and will teach you to take your ability to a much higher level.

Often when you suggest one legged skiing to people you receive looks of disbelief in response - people thinking to themselves "there's no way I am going to be able to do that". At the beginning it can be difficult to balance on a single ski, but one legged skiing has a quick learning curve and most

CARVING
ONE LEGGED SKIING
- **BALANCE DEVELOPMENT**
- **THIGH DRIVING**
- **CARVING ON ONE LEG**

skiers show a massive improvement after only 10 or 15 minutes of practice. When you first try to ski on just one leg make sure you find a shallow terrain. It is easier to make turns with a shorter radius when you are only wearing one ski. Try to get some rhythm into the turns and also use a stronger than normal pole plant to help you maintain your balance at first (**fig. 46**). And be sure to practise one legged skiing in each direction.

fig. 46 - pole plant adds balance

THIGH DRIVING

A major factor you should bear in mind when you attempt one legged skiing is that it is harder to turn in one direction than the other.

It will feel relatively easy when the leg with the ski on is the downhill ski, or the outside leg, in the turn. However, when that leg and ski becomes the inside leg and ski during the next turn, it becomes a lot more difficult to balance and steer the ski through the turn - and you will need to work a lot harder steering and leaning the leg into the turn. This is where the real skill of one legged skiing develops.

During the difficult part of the turn it helps to think about thigh driving - another technique that was discussed in Handbook 1. You can simulate thigh driving from a static position. Lift your knee up across your body and then drive it across the thigh (**fig. 47**). You will need the same movement when you are

fig. 47 - thigh driving from a static position

CARVING

skiing on one leg when you are steering the ski on your inside leg.

Once you have worked on this movement you should feel more confident steering the ski through the turn when the ski is on the inside leg (**fig. 48**).

fig. 48 - thigh driving = strong inside leg

CARVING ON ONE LEG

As you become more confident at steering in both directions while skiing on one leg, try to gradually steer more and increase the lean of your leg so that you begin to carve your turns. This requires an even more precise level of balance. Allow your speed to increase slightly so you start to lean more across the ski. It is important that you are confident

and do not increase your speed too quickly so that you progressively develop the range of movement in leaning across the ski when it is on the inside of the turn. Eventually you should be able to ski at your normal speed and feel that your turns are controlled and have a good turn shape.

CARVING - A SUMMARY

To successfully carve faster you need to adopt a wider, more open and lower symmetrical stance.

Softening, flexing and increasing the lean of your inner leg will allow your legs to lean together and the edge angles to increase.

Your crossover from one ski to the other needs to be dynamic - and not a delayed or upward movement.

At higher speeds you have less time to react to changes in the terrain or other skiers, so you need to increase your awareness.

Any rotation of arms, shoulders or hips puts you in a weaker position. Keeping your hands inside your elbows and within your peripheral vision can prevent rotation.

Every skier prefers turning in one direction to the other. Differences can be evened out by practising exercises on the weaker side.

Skiing on one leg can help improve your overall balance.

STEEPS

INTRODUCTION TO STEEPS

As your level of ability improves, so does your desire to ski steeper slopes. Handbook 1 introduced you to the changes it is necessary to make to your stance and your technique to ski steeper slopes. Through practising the tips, examples and exercises outlined in Handbook 1 you should have increased confidence in tackling steeper gradients.

This chapter focuses on four key ways in which you can take your steeps technique to the next level - again with tips, examples and exercises to help you.

A
ANKLE FLEX
DEVELOPMENT

UNDERSTAND FLEX PATTERN

One of the biggest problems faced by most intermediate and advanced skiers when they are skiing steep slopes is an insufficient range of ankle flex movement. Just as when they are carving, skiers find it more difficult to flex their ankle joints than their knee or hip joints (**fig. 49**).

**fig. 49 - 80% knee,
20% ankle**

There are several reasons for this. Firstly, ski boots feel rigid and alien from the first day you put them on when you start skiing. The boots almost feel that they are not actually designed to flex.

Secondly, it can be intimidating to travel downhill when you first start skiing. The easiest joint to flex is the knee joint, and you may feel you are safer when you flex it. This is not necessarily the case, but it is difficult to override such instinctive feelings.

Thirdly your ski instructor is likely to have told you repeatedly when you were learning to ski to "bend ze knees" - this normally scares you into flexing the knee joint. Finally many skiers ski in boots that are too rigid for them, which makes the ankle joint lack flexibility. This lack of ankle flex can cause fundamental problems with overall technique.

Leverage

One of the main problems with a lack of ankle flex is that you have less leverage in the legs to steer and turn the skis - the less leverage you have the less power you have.

A good comparison to make is to arm wrestling. Imagine you are

trying to wrestle somebody with an almost straight arm that lacks flex. In contrast the person you are wrestling with has a very flexed arm - they would easily win even if they were only half your size (**fig. 50**).

fig. 50 - arm wrestling with a straight arm

If you lack the necessary leverage in your legs to steer the skis you will have to look elsewhere for the power. The next best parts of the body to do the steering are the hips and then the shoulders - but if you use these parts of the body they will generally rotate, which results in a weaker skiing stance.

Back Seat

The other problem you get if the flex in the ankle is not equal to the flex in the knee is that every time you flex up and down on your skis your body weight is not positioned over the middle of the skis. The weight of the body will move to the back of the skis (**fig. 51**).

fig. 51 - weight on the back of the skis

As a result the skis are harder to steer and not only will you not have the necessary leverage but you will need to put in almost 10 times the effort to turn the skis.

TEST MECHANICS AND RANGE

It is a good idea to identify the correct set-up for ankle flex while standing on the spot. Start by trying to stand as tall as you can through the legs and fully extend the ankle and knee joints. Then slowly flex down towards the

ground and see how low you can go while driving the knees forwards along the line of the ski, aiming to get the knee towards or even over the binding on your ski. Develop this on both sides until you feel you have increased the range of movement in your ankle flex (**fig. 52**).

fig. 52 - ankle flex = hip and knee flex

Something that you will probably work out as you are practising this movement is that you don't actually have to think about flexing the knee joint at all. When you concentrate on flexing the ankle joint alone, the knee joint flexes naturally. Furthermore the flex in the knee will be the correct amount so that your body weight is over the middle of the skis and is not placed too far back.

ANKLE FLEX TURNING

Once you have worked out the correct flex pattern for the ankle joint and have a better understanding as to why it is such an essential part of your skiing foundation, it is time to practise and develop exercises to build the strength and skill of the ankle. The best way to do this is to isolate the ankle and force it into making the whole movement of a turn from start to finish on just one leg (**fig. 53**).

fig. 53 - ankle isolation

EXERCISE 6
ANKLE FLEX TURNING

THE AIM
**To build the
strength and skill
of the ankle flex.**

WHERE
Start on a flattish slope to begin with.

How
First, standing on your uphill leg, repeat the flexing movement you have just tried while standing on the spot. This will ensure that you have the right amount of flex in the ankle joint so that you know you will have enough leverage to steer the ski. Make sure you are standing on the uphill leg, as it is about to become your new downhill or outside leg (**fig. 54**).

**fig. 54 - uphill leg to
downhill leg**

Once you have determined you have enough flex in the ankle, start to power the ski through to steer the ski from the start to the finish of the turn (**fig. 55**). Be sure to keep the other leg off the ground until you have completed the turn (**fig. 56**). The

**fig. 55 - powering through
the turn**

temptation for many skiers is to put the other ski down on the surface before they have completed the turn. At first this exercise may feel quite difficult, but if you persevere with it you will get results. Make sure that you practise the exercise in both directions, to increase the strength and skill of both ankles.

fig. 56 - complete the turn

The Result

After some practice the ankle joint will feel stronger and more flexible, which will bring new found strength to the turn.

ANKLE FLEX HOPPING AND JUMPING

When you feel you can complete the turn on just one leg using the new found leverage and flexibility of the ankle joint, start to develop the ankle flex further. This can be done by 'hopping' yourself around the turn - this is a great way to test the maximum flexing capabilities of your ankle joints.

You will need the same pattern of ankle flex as you had in Exercise 6, but this time with even more power and reactive force - enough of both so that you can actually jump the ski off the ground. Further flex in the ankle is also needed to ensure that your landing after the 'hop' is soft and does not cause too much of a shock to the body.

Once you feel confident that you have the right amount of flex in the ankle, try to jump around the turn (**fig. 57**). After some practice you will be able to hop through a full 180 degrees from left to right and you will have increased the flex in your ankle and improved the

leverage you have to steer and turn the skis, especially in steeper, more challenging environments.

fig. 57 - 'hopping' around the turn

B
THIGH HIGH

The concept of 'Thigh High' was considered in Handbook 1 - as a way to increase ankle flex and to put the hips over the balls of the feet. This section considers further how thinking 'Thigh High' can improve your steep slope technique.

```
    STEEPS
    THIGH HIGH
●   MANUAL ADJUSTMENT
```

MANUAL ADJUSTMENT

A problem skiers commonly have when they are steep slope skiing is that they do not react enough to changes in the gradient and make the necessary adjustments to their body to adapt to any increase in the steepness.

Many skiers adopt the position that they use on a slope with a gradient of 20 degrees and ski in that position even though the gradient of the slope is now 35 degrees (**fig. 58**). Skiers are often held back from adjusting to the steeper gradient because of a fear of moving their hips further down the hill, the thought of which can be very intimidating. The best way to get the body into the correct position for steep slopes, just as with carving, is to think 'Thigh High' (**fig. 59**).

**fig. 58 - thigh angle
the same, slope
angle different**

**fig. 59 - thigh angle
adjusted to match
the gradient**

**EXERCISE 7
THINK THIGH HIGH**

THE AIM
To raise the angle
of the thighs to
match the gradient
of the slope.

WHERE
As a steep slope may feel too intimidating, first make some turns down a slope with a lesser gradient.

HOW
The way to adjust your position is to stand taller using just the angle of the thigh and retaining the flex in the ankle and upper body (**fig. 60**). Until you get used to the feeling this may feel a bit strange and not very dynamic, but persevere with it. Move to a slope with a steeper gradient after you have got used to the adjustments you have made and you have successfully made a few turns down a gentle slope (**fig. 61**).

THE RESULT
You should feel more in control and better set up to cope with an increase in the gradient.

fig. 60 - thigh high and
ankle flex

fig. 61 - ...and the same on
a steeper slope

C

TAIL RELEASE

STEEPS
TAIL RELEASE
● GETTING A FEEL FOR IT
● TAKE IT TO THE STEEPS

GETTING A FEEL FOR IT

Skiers often catch the tails of their skis in the snow when they are skiing steep slopes. This can also happen when they are skiing gentler slopes, but the steeper the slope becomes the more likely it is to happen. You can still catch the very tail end of the ski in the snow even when you feel you have set up the turn correctly, projected forwards and down the hill and raised your skis off the ground (**fig. 62**).

fig. 62 - tail end of ski catches

A useful tip for avoiding this is to make a 'Tail Release' as you initiate the turn - by slightly raising the tails of the skis off the surface of the snow. This can help skiers who have trouble making turns on steep slopes and always find that the tail end of the ski catches and can also help those skiers who have more experience skiing steep slopes but who are trying to negotiate an awkward bit of terrain.

To begin with, practise the tail release manoeuvre on less steep terrain, so that you get a feel for it. As you initiate the turn, plant your pole and start to project your legs and body upwards so that your skis leave the surface of the snow. As you start to leave the ground or become almost weightless, try to feel that you are pulling your heels up towards your lower back (**fig. 63**). Your heels will not actually get as far as your lower back but they will raise themselves further off the ground than normal, and this movement will change the angle of the ski enough to clear the tails of the surface (**fig. 64**).

TAKE IT TO THE STEEPS

Try this tail manoeuvre out on steeper terrain when you have

fig. 63 - pulling heels upwards

fig. 64 - the tails of the skis leave the ground

practised it a few times. Be sure to plant your pole positively to support yourself and then extend your legs and body once more, tucking your heels up underneath you as you go. This manoeuvre can actually be quite good fun and can make you realise that you can move your skis more than you ever thought you could.

D
HOLDING THE EDGE

When skiing steep slopes, many skiers put a lot of effort into initiating and executing each turn but then find that the edge of the ski breaks away at the end of the turn. Skiers who are inexperienced on steep slopes can find it difficult to get the edges of the skis to grip to the surface at this stage. Holding the edges on steep slopes so that they grip the snow can be quite difficult. It requires a good level of skill and sensitivity to use your edges correctly, especially as the pressure builds up in the last part of the turn.

SIMULTANEOUS EDGE CHECKING

Whatever your level of skiing, it is good to learn to 'check' your ski edges against the snow. This halts the speed at which you ski - which is essential for steep slope skiing. To 'check' successfully, both edges need to grip the snow simultaneously. To achieve this you need to lean your legs more and together into the hill. Many skiers only lean their downhill leg into the hill - while

STEEPS
HOLDING THE EDGE
- **SIMULTANEOUS EDGE CHECKING**
- **DOWNWARDS PRESSURE**

the inside leg remains rigid (**fig. 65**). To get used to this, practise edge checking on a shallower gradient, so that your confidence and skill can develop - and practise the movement repeatedly in both directions. Once you have mastered 'checking' on a gentle gradient, move to a steeper slope. Work hard on driving both legs into the hill, not just the downhill leg (**fig. 66**).

fig. 65 - bad edge angles

fig. 66 - good edge angles

When you feel that you are checking the edge of the downhill ski and the edge of the uphill ski simultaneously, try to develop further the athleticism of the movement. If you can build the edge check into a stronger and more solid movement, it will make your turn more dynamic. To achieve this you need to think about driving the side of your thighs into the hill while keeping your upper body and hips facing down the hill. When you feel you are ready, put this into practice during a complete run of turns and you should feel a difference in the increased level of control that you now have.

DOWNWARDS PRESSURE

Now you understand how to get the edges to check into the snow, it is worth turning your attention to how you handle the build up of pressure as the skis go through the turn. At the half way point of the turn on the steep slopes you will notice how the pressure starts to build up underneath the feet. Because the slope is steeper, and as a result usually icier, you have to be very skilful to maintain the edge hold. Though it is tempting to try and push away the pressure under the feet, try to avoid doing this. Skiers often feel the need to brake on steeper slopes, and if they start to panic, the normal reaction is to push against the downhill ski. If you do this the edge of the ski will break away from the surface of the snow and the ski will skid down the hill (**fig. 67**).

**fig. 68 - delicate
downwards pressure**

**fig. 67 - too much pressure
causes the edge to break away**

As you go into the second half of the turn try to think of the build up of downwards pressure as delicate - just as if you were standing on the tips of your toes. This will help you not to push away the downhill ski and help you to maintain a pressure on the edge that is directly down into the snow (**fig. 68**).

STEEPS - A SUMMARY

An insufficient range of ankle flex inhibits successful steep slope skiing.

Improving ankle flex increases the leverage you have to steer the ski and ensures that your weight is positioned over the middle of the ski.

Reacting to changes in the gradient and making necessary adjustments to your body gives you more control on steeper slopes.

To get the correct position for steep slope skiing, think 'Thigh High'.

Making a 'Tail Release' as you initiate a turn stops the tail end of the ski catching in the snow.

On the steep slopes a positive pole plant provides support.

Maintaining the edge grip of the skis against the snow throughout the whole turn gives you more control.

Simultaneously 'checking' your edges and keeping a delicate pressure on the edges helps to increase the grip your skis have on the snow.

MOGULS

INTRODUCTION TO MOGULS

Handbook 1 introduced the four key ways in which to improve your technique when skiing moguls. By now you should have enough confidence and ability to get amongst the moguls, through practice of the tips, examples and exercises outlined in Handbook 1.

This chapter focuses on four further ways in which you can take your mogul technique to the next level - with further tips, examples and exercises to help you.

A
SPEED CONTROL

As with skiing steep slopes, moguls are more enjoyable the more control that you have.

GETTING FAZED

If there is one thing that fazes most skiers it is skiing moguls, as looked at in Handbook 1 - whether the skier is venturing into moguls for the first time or even if the skier has some experience tackling steeper or icier moguls. An essential element of skiing moguls successfully is being able to control your speed. First, this will help to stop you being fazed by the moguls, and secondly it will help you to develop your skills so you are able to ski steeper and more difficult mogul fields. It is useful to develop those elements of ski technique that will give you speed control, as this will lead to general improvements in your overall ability, which in turn will give you the confidence to learn and progress further in all disciplines.

> **MOGULS**
> **SPEED CONTROL**
> ● **GETTING FAZED**
> ● **AUTO EDGE**
> ● **SKID FOR CONTROL**

AUTO EDGE

One of the biggest problems skiers face when trying to ski moguls is the way in which the skis accelerate after they have made one or two turns. Stopping your skis from accelerating in this way is a habit that is hard to break, as the majority of the turns that you make when you ski on piste require you to edge your skis to keep control. The same is not true for moguls - the way in which you would angle your edges, known as the 'edge set', for carving on piste is not the best one to use (**fig. 69**).

fig. 69 - usual edge angles

To control your speed in the moguls, the first thing you must do is become aware of how much you automatically angle the skis so

that they edge and then try to adjust the angle of the skis so that you execute each turn with very little edge (**fig. 70**).

fig. 70 - reduced edging allows sideslip

SKID FOR CONTROL

You will notice straight away that your skis do not accelerate through the turn if you reduce the angle of your edges, or if you flatten the skis more against the surface of the slope. In fact the turn becomes more predictable and as a result you will feel you have more control - even though your skis are actually skidding. To get used to the sensation of skidding, practise the movement across a piste until you feel comfortable and confident with it.

MOGULS

When you reach this point, take your newly developed skidding technique into the moguls. You should feel more relaxed and have more time to actually think about skiing the moguls rather than just surviving in them (**fig. 71**).

**fig. 71 - from survival
to enjoyment**

B
FINDING A LINE

Often when skiing moguls, skiers get frustrated because they struggle to find and maintain a line to get through the moguls. Consequently they lose the rhythm of their descent. This usually happens for two reasons: first, some skiers lack the skill to adjust their technique to cope with the terrain, and as a result they are unable to move as required to get from one mogul to another, particularly when the bumps are irregularly placed. The other reason is that they do not know, and so can not use, certain useful tactics that would help them to find their way through a mogul field (**fig. 72**).

**fig. 72 - regular descent
down the fall line**

MOGULS

SKILFUL SKIDDING

Moguls are not always made or placed in a perfect line, so you need to be able to vary the skidding movement of your skis and manoeuvre yourself according to their make-up and position - and at the same time keep a decent rhythm flowing.

**EXERCISE 8
SKIDDING**

**THE AIM
To get used to
changing the edge
set to a skidding
movement.**

WHERE
On a piste on which you feel comfortable.

HOW
While descending the piste, vary the skidding movement so that you are not just skidding in a set pattern - skid directly down and across the slope, and even try to skid backwards (**fig. 73**).

fig. 73 - altering skidding pattern on piste...

When you feel you can adjust your skidding movement to get you successfully down the whole slope, try to introduce a higher level of athleticism into the movement. This will help you develop further the level of your skidding skill and enable you to better adapt your technique to irregularly made and placed moguls. When you feel you have made some progress on the piste take this higher skill level into a mogul field (**fig. 74**).

fig. 74 - ...and taking it into the moguls

MOGULS

THE RESULT

When you have mastered controlled skidding, your descents through irregular moguls will flow better and will stop and start less. The development of your skidding skill will help you find a nicer mogul line more easily - and stay more directly in the fall line of the mogul field (fig. 75).

fig. 75 - straight down
the fall line

TACTICS

There are a few other tactics you can use to help you find a line through the moguls. To start with you can simply use your vision. Think about looking further ahead - not just one or two bumps in front of you but 5, 6 or even 7. This will give you a better idea of how you need to adapt your technique for what lies ahead (**fig. 76**).

mogul skiing and keep using them until they become second nature (**fig. 77**).

fig. 77 - four points are better than two

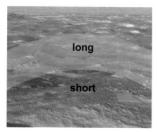

fig. 76 - short vision, long vision

Another way to find a line is to walk your poles down the hill and make good positive pole plants with them. Having four points of contact working for you, both hands as well as both feet, helps you to manoeuvre yourself more easily through the moguls. Incorporate these tactics into your

C

RHYTHM

A key element of mogul skiing is rhythm. Rhythm is very important for the flow of your descent and to help you get a feel for the terrain on which you are skiing. To improve your descent down through the moguls, you can use your pole plant to add and develop rhythm.

Skiers quite often neglect their pole plant, and do not regard it as an important factor of good skiing. Instead most skiers just rely on their feet. However, the more advanced your skiing becomes, especially for all terrain skiing, the more important your pole plant becomes (**fig. 78**).

**fig. 78 - a good pole plant
is invaluable**

**EXERCISE 9
POLE PLANTING FOR
RHYTHM**

THE AIM
To develop your
pole plant to add
rhythm to your
mogul skiing.

fig. 79 - tick...

WHERE
Use a gradient that is steep enough to warrant using a pole plant, such as a blue or red run.

HOW
First, to get an idea of the rhythm of your pole plant and how good it is, practise making short radius turns on piste. Really test yourself and see if you can make pole plants for a reasonable number of turns with exactly the same rhythm throughout the descent (**fig. 79 & 80**). It is not as easy as it sounds. If you stumble or lose your balance slightly while you are skiing, the rhythm of your pole plant is normally affected.

You need to practise this exercise to develop your pole planting skills to a level where it will not be affected even if you lose your balance or rhythm as you ski. This increase in skill will also

fig. 80 - ...tock

MOGULS

help you to get back into balance more quickly.

When you feel you have developed an increased level of rhythm in your pole plant, try it out in the moguls.

THE RESULT
Your descent has more feeling and rhythm and flows better (fig. 81).

fig. 81 - a more flowing descent

D
AVOIDING MID-BODY BREAK

MOGULS
AVOIDING MID-BODY BREAK

Another common problem skiers have when skiing moguls is that their waist or middle body folds over or 'breaks' when they ski into the mogul (**fig. 82**). To overcome this you have to learn to ski with a slightly stronger middle body. Most of us already have enough strength in our stomach muscles to do this without going to the gym. The key factor is to combine the other aspects required in a good mogul technique and also remain strong in the stomach whilst you are skiing.

fig. 82 - weak core = mid-body break

**EXERCISE 10
MIDDLE BODY
STRENGTH**

**THE AIM
To stop the waist
from breaking.**

fig. 83 - 'hop'

WHERE
On a slope on which you feel comfortable.

How
Make a series of turns down the slope and put in a small hop between each turn (**fig. 83**). As you land, focus on keeping the middle of your body strong and do not allow it to break at the waist. Also think about keeping the upper part of your body strong and un-fazed by the landing. To achieve this, keep your shoulders slightly up and focus on preparing the core muscles in your stomach so they can anticipate the landing. With time you will train your middle body and make it much less vulnerable to breaking (**fig. 84**).

THE RESULT
If you apply this when you ski moguls your descents will be much more consistent.

fig. 84 - strong core = upper body support

MOGULS - A SUMMARY

Mogul skiing is one thing that fazes most skiers.

Only very little edge is required for mogul skiing.

Less edge causes the skis to flatten and results in a skidding movement, which makes turns through the moguls more predictable.

Finding a line through the moguls will make your descents more flowing, and mean you stop and start less.

Looking further ahead and using a positive pole plant will help you find a line through the moguls.

Rhythm is a key element of mogul skiing.

A positive pole plant is an essential element of rhythm.

Retaining some tension in your stomach muscles - to prevent the waist or middle body from breaking - will give you more control.

FREERIDE

INTRODUCTION TO FREERIDE

Handbook 1 looked at how freeride, powder and off-piste skiing requires adaptability for success.

This chapter focuses on four key ways in which to further adapt your technique so you are prepared for any conditions. Again the tips, examples and exercises will help you improve your freeriding and off-piste skiing and make even more of the mountain accessible.

A

SHOCK ABSORBING
SYSTEM

**FREERIDE
SHOCK ABSORBING
SYSTEM**

One of the obvious differences between freeskiing and on piste skiing is the terrain. On piste the terrain is usually groomed and very predictable. Freeskiing terrain is as it sounds - free and only groomed by the elements. Freeskiing is generally more demanding than on piste skiing because the terrain is always changing and throwing in some surprises, which can 'shock' the legs and body (**fig. 85**).

fig. 85 - 'shocked' legs

When freeskiing it is not unusual to find sudden compressions in the terrain - such as a slope that just drops away and down half a metre, or bumpy harder snow or the odd 'cookie' hidden in the snow. All of these factors can shock the legs and can result in you being thrown off balance.

To survive the condition changes that occur when you are freeskiing you need to develop a good shock absorbing system, to allow your legs to take the pressure that hits the skis if you suddenly come across a compression in the terrain - or they have to deal with a loss of pressure as the terrain suddenly drops away. As with carving, we can use an analogy with a car. It is the shock absorbers in cars that help you to drive smoothly whatever the conditions of the road. The shock absorbers work hard to deal with the changes in pressure on the tyres and wheels - their ultimate purpose is to give the passenger a smooth ride. Your legs should work in the same way as shock absorbers to protect and give your upper body a smooth ride when freeskiing.

One way to help develop this feeling in your legs is to try to keep a constant pressure against the

surface on which you are skiing. Try to imagine that you are continually pushing against the snow with the bottom of your skis (**fig. 86**).

fig. 86 - push against the snow

If something hits your legs you need to be ready to absorb the shock and push the legs straight back out. A lot of the time skiers are slow to react after a compression, and do not push their legs back out against the surface so they lose contact straight after they have hit a compression.

The same principle applies when you come across the opposite of a compression or a bump and the slope actually drops away a little. You need to be able to react quickly and be ready to extend your legs back out again to ensure that your skis stay in contact with the surface of the snow. If you spend a little time thinking about this and put in some practice, you should eventually get a better feel for changes in the terrain and be able to absorb the shocks better, the result of which will be a smoother ride (**fig. 87**).

fig. 87 - a smoother ride

B
POLE WALKING

**FREERIDE
POLE WALKING**

When you are freeskiing, particularly in powder snow, the next turn sometimes feels like it is going to happen in no man's land - you are not always sure what lies ahead or if the snow texture is going to be different within a short distance of 5 or 10 metres from where you are skiing at that moment. The texture and condition of powder and other snow that you may come across while freeskiing can vary greatly - including wind packed snow, snow with a crust on top, perfect light powder, spring snow and heavy slush.

When conditions vary in this way it helps to know within a split second what type of snow lies ahead of you so that you can adapt your stance and approach to react accordingly. A good technique to use is 'Pole Walking' - which is just one of the reasons that an effective pole plant is an essential tool for freeskiing. When 'Pole Walking' you basically make consistent pole plants for the whole descent - as if they were second nature. Walking your poles down the hill gives you more feedback as to what conditions you will encounter as you make the turn. The contact that the pole makes with the snow as it swings forwards at the start of the turn can be passed onto your brain as feedback on the conditions. Within this split second of contact you get all the information you need to know what kind of conditions your skis are about to ride over (**fig. 88**).

**fig. 88 - information from
pole to brain**

In addition, this feedback from your poles will give you more confidence and help you to develop your all mountain technique.

C
TAKING AIR

How many times have you been skiing in powder and had to stop a descent or alter the course of your run because it involved a small jump? Have you ever tried to make a small jump while skiing in powder so that your friend can take a picture of you? But it all went badly wrong, with you becoming an instant snowman with goggles in one place and skis and poles in another?

If that sounds familiar you will appreciate how being able to negotiate changes in the terrain and jump if necessary is a useful way to broaden your skills for freeskiing. The best way to learn how to jump is by trying out the basic technique on small jumps in the controlled and predictable environment of a snow park.

You should think about 'popping' off the jump as you take off. Many skiers make the mistake of just skiing off the jump and then practically sit down as they take off. This causes their weight to go back and they usually end up wiping out. To make sure you 'pop' off the jump, practise extending your legs down and projecting your body upwards (**fig. 89**).

fig. 89 - legs extended, 'popping' on take-off

fig. 90 - eyes forward, hands forward, prepare to 'stomp'

The next thing you should think about at this stage is keeping your vision up. There is a common tendency for skiers to look down as they go off a jump. Lowering your vision like this causes your weight to go back and again can make you lose your balance. To prevent this from happening, keep your vision up and look forward towards where you want to land. Keep your hands forwards as you go through the air (**fig. 90**).

The last thing to think about is 'stomping' your landing. To do this, your body and legs need to be strong and flexible when your skis touch the surface - they should not be loose or weak. If your body is too loose or weak it will collapse down and cause you to sit back. Your thighs need to have the same strength in them as they would need if you were trying to stand up from a squat while working out in the gym.

When you have practised the basics of jumping and have the foundation of the technique required, try to incorporate jumps into your descent when you next have the opportunity to take a little bit of air when you are freeskiing.

D
WIND AFFECTED SNOW

SNOW DIFFERENCES

There is a major difference between light powder snow that fell during calm conditions and new snow that was affected by high winds as it fell. When snow falls during windy conditions it gets firmly compacted. Consequently rather than feeling soft and forgiving, the snow becomes quite hard and it is not so easy to absorb your skis into it.

When fresh snow is like this you need to take a different approach to skiing through it. The firmness of the snow means that you have got to work a lot harder to ski it well. You need to adapt the way in which you ski so that you are 'powering' through your turns.

POWER TURNING

Power Turning can be achieved by really forcing your legs out from underneath you and using them to keep a constant pressure against and into the snow. As the snow will be difficult to turn into when it is compacted you need to allow yourself to rise above the surface of the snow when you start to turn (**fig. 91**).

The amount of power you need to be able to push the skis back through the firm surface of the snow is about twice as much as you normally need when skiing on piste or in light powder - it is a little like going to the gym and stacking a couple of extra blocks on the weights machine.

If you power your legs to this degree you will find yourself moving through the firmly packed and windblown snow and you will begin to enjoy what would otherwise have been a nightmare run.

fig. 91 - rise above the turn

As you come above the snow, prepare your legs to drive your skis back into the snow to round off the turn (**fig. 92**).

fig. 92 - legs driving into turn with extra power

FREERIDE - A SUMMARY

Freeskiing terrain is more unpredictable and consequently more demanding than pisted slopes.

The legs need to develop a good shock absorbing system to deal with sudden changes in the terrain such as compressions or different snow conditions.

An effective pole plant is an essential tool for freeskiing, as it provides feedback to the brain on the conditions ahead of you.

Being able to jump broadens your freeskiing skills.

A snowpark is the best environment in which to learn jumping skills.

Three rules of jumping are: 'popping off', 'vision up' and 'stomping the landing'.

The type of snow dictates the technique you use - light powder snow is easier to ski than wind affected snow.

A FINAL WORD

We hope you have learned something from the images, explanations and exercises in this book. Whether you are looking at performance carving, steep slopes, hitting the moguls or freeskiing in glorious powder, use the exercises to develop your skill level. Don't just try them once when you are away skiing, especially if you are having a bad day, also try them at your local dry ski slope or snow slope. Using these types of development drills in this way you can improve your skill level before you hit the mountains. Keep the ideas in your head, or make notes and keep the book on you when you go skiing so you can re-cap on the points and jog your memory. Combined practise will make you into a good all mountain skier.

Good luck with changing your skiing and hopefully catch up with you at the Academy in Verbier in the winter or Saas-Fee in the summer.

All the best
Warren Smith

Index

INDEX

APPENDIX OF EXERCISES

CARVING

STEEPS

MOGULS

let warren look after your skiing...

VBR

verbier

the snowmole guide

val de bagnes

"indispensable for skiers and
boarders alike"
Richard Cowper, Financial Times

by isobel rostron & michael kayson

aurants-directories-bars-resort information-new style piste m

THE WARREN SMITH SKI ACADEMY HANDBOOK SERIES

The Warren Smith Ski Academy - Academy Handbook 1 is also available to buy, from major outdoor retailers and major bookstores, and direct from the Warren Smith Ski Academy. Handbook 3 in the series will be available soon.

LESSON 1
£9.99

LESSON 3
£9.99

THE WARREN SMITH SKI ACADEMY DVD SERIES

The successful formula used by the Warren Smith Ski Academy to build confidence and skill development is available on DVD. Designed to help intermediates, advanced and expert skiers they are recommended by Ski & Board, the Daily Mail Ski & Snowboard, the London Ski Show, The Sunday Times, The Mail on Sunday, the Independent on Sunday, Capital Radio, ITV, Men's Health, Esquire and ifyouski.com

Priced at £16.99, the DVD is available from major outdoor retailers. The DVDs can be ordered on the Mail Order Hotline (+44 (0)1525 374757) or by email (sales@snowsportsynergy.com). Visa and MasterCard accepted. Mail Order guarantees delivery within 2 or 3 days.

LESSON 1 gives solutions for Carving, Steeps, Moguls and Freeskiing, with technical explanations, exercises and skill development for the 4 topics to help you become a confident all mountain skiers. There is also a special freeride safety explanation by top British guide Nick Parks, additional footage on 'Ski Biomechanics', 'Physiology', 'Ski Maintenance' and the actual script written by Warren for the programme.

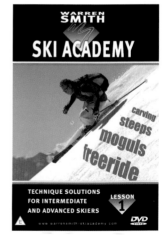

LESSON 2 continues on from where Lesson 1 left off. Once again split into Carving, Steeps, Moguls and Freeride, there are more exercises, tips, and explanations to help you to take your skiing to the next level. As with Lesson 1, the learning process is progressive and works under the philosophy of matching skill development with confidence building. DVD Extras include 'Skier Cross training', 'Ski Biomechanics continued', 'Safety Check', 'Pilates Core Strength Training Off Skis', 'Mountain Bike' and the script for the programme.

LESSON 3 gives intermediate, advanced and expert technique solutions for Carving, Steeps, Moguls and Freeskiing (powder/off-piste). It is also designed to aid 'GAP year ski instructor' level skiers. DVD extras include 'Dry Land Training', 'on Mountain Warm-Up', 'Skiercross Introduction' and 'More Mountain Bike'.

THE WARREN SMITH SKI ACADEMY

Based in Verbier, Switzerland, courses at the Warren Smith Ski Academy cater for intermediate, advance and expert skiers. The concept of the courses is to build an individual's skill and confidence to enable them to ski the whole mountain and not be restricted by terrain.

Courses and camps cover a wide range of the skiing spectrum - Personal Performance, Freeride/Powder, New School Freestyle, Heliskiing, Moguls, Race Training, Instructor Training, and Biomechanics - and you can choose which area to concentrate on if you wish. You can also be advised on what might be best for you.

GROUP COURSES last for 5 days (10am-3pm) and cover the main topics of Moguls, Powder, Steeps and Carving. Skills are developed during the course by practising specific exercises that benefit the main topics. The new levels of skill are progressively tested on suitable terrain to build confidence. As all skiers have different strengths and weaknesses each skier is looked at individually. Video Analysis is used 1-2 times during the course depending on weather conditions. An analysis of ski equipment is also part of the course, to educate skiers on how to get more out of their kit and understand it in greater depth.

PRIVATE COACHING is also available upon request, for a full day (10am-3pm) or a half day (10am-12:30pm or 1pm-3:30pm). The content of the private coaching is specific to what the client wants to do and what the client needs to work on.

Contact:
The Warren Smith Ski Academy, A Snowsport Synergy Ltd company
UK Office: +44 (0)1525 374757
Swiss Office: +41 (0)79 359 6566
Website: www.warrensmith-skiacademy.com
Email: admin@snowsportsynergy.com

THE WARREN SMITH ACADEMY TEAM

The Warren Smith Ski Academy brings together some of the sports top professionals to create the ultimate coaching team guaranteeing ski technique solutions. Success is achieved by evolving traditional methods of coaching and focusing on the enjoyment and adrenaline factor. Skier Confidence is increased as levels of skill are developed. Awareness of new ski technology is raised at the Academy, showing skiers how to get greater sensations and more from their equipment.

Full profiles of the Academy Team members are available on the Academy website - www.warrensmith-skiacademy.com

GAP YEAR COURSE

The Warren Smith Ski Academy also runs a GAP year program in association with BASI (www.basi.org.uk). The program runs for nine weeks in the prestigious resort of Verbier and takes students up to BASI 3 ski instructor level.

For more information of the GAP year course send an email to warrensmith@snowsportsynergy.com or call 01525 374757.

CARVING NOTES

Steeps Notes

MOGULS NOTES

FREERIDE NOTES